She Who Sings Is Not Always Happy

b

Julia Usman

She Who Sings Is Not Always Happy

First published in paperback format by
Coverstory books, 2021

ISBN 978-1-8382321-3-9

Cover illustration is "Steps Wood"
© Jill Eagle, 2018.

www.coverstorybooks.com

to Dad (1933-2014)
for passing on his love of books

Contents

Foreword

I first met Julia Usman on a Poetry Masterclass course at Ty Newydd in North Wales. We talked about how we were drawn to writing about nature, particularly the environment directly around us. I was fascinated to hear about her experience of living and working on a farm while raising her children; there's a vicarious pleasure to be gained from hearing about a life different from one's own, in particular through the eyes of another woman, one who is also a mother and a writer.

Usman's life in her homeland of North Yorkshire, her travels, and later on, her life in Dubai, form a backdrop of contrasting terrain, but changing landscape is also an ongoing theme within this collection, of not only the exterior world but also of the heart. One might assume that the subject matter of these poems is autobiographical. In 'Mothering', trust builds between woman and a lame ewe, but ultimately, "She longs to take off her keen-worn hands / the loose gold circle that binds her to this farm", in 'Wife'. And then there's the frisson of new love in 'Lost' on seeing a glove she writes "I can slip the yellow courage of a hand inside / touch the red glow of my blush".

The poetry in this collection is wonderfully sparse, often cut to a minimum but well-refined. This makes for a directness where the reader is taken straight to the crux of a poem. Such brevity, like daubs on a canvas, will leave you wanting more, but there is always room for the reader to let their own imagination flow allowing the poems to resonate for longer, their voice ringing out across hillside and wadi.

As I have discovered myself, the process of creating poems can be a tantalising one, sometimes out of reach, even to the writer. In 'Time Machine' she writes, "I have a pen fountain blue / it writes the past / as it lies beside / this window / looking out across fells / that are free / from all words". The title of the collection, *She Who Sings Is Not Always Happy*, perhaps tells us more. It can seem as if all is laid out in plain sight and yet there is complexity and mystery within this simplicity. Usman's first collection is far more than its parts.

Alison Lock

Time machine

today I have a pen
fountain blue
it writes the past
as it lies beside
this window
looking out across fells
that are free
from all words
I sometimes wonder
what the pen calls itself

tomorrow it will write
the future
a nib that defies full-stops
I envy this pen
suspended in a space
it knows nothing about

Dorothy's song

Her voice
is a quiet feather
a fractured window
in winter sun
a wind-borne shiver
of crab blossom
celandine, sycamore
oak, a communion
over Silver How.
She is a shepherd
gathering him
down from the fells
a Bird nesting
under a blind moon
the North Star at noon
lost in blue
her song
half hidden
half whole.

"Her voice was like a hidden Bird", taken from 'Home at Grasmere'
William Wordsworth

Imagining Ophelia

Tonight, I dream of drowning,
wade out towards your shadow
blind to our light on water.
My breath washed downstream
bound to the banks of our estuary
never reaching the sea.
This black hole of a rainbow
that swallows the shore
anchors tight
into pockets of stones.
Caught in a confluence
the lace on my sleeves
cannot float enough to save me.
I welcome the silt and eddy
waist deep, roped to reeds
the moon swallowed by the river.

A dark-haired woman

I keep thinking of Maggie
in the attic, attacking
her doll with nails
severing the beauty.
Maggie coiled around debris
her impetuous flesh
more animal than girl
more water than woman.
Maggie wearing her darkest veil
hiding the nails inside her head.

"I'm determined to read no more books where the blond-haired women carry away all the happiness"- George Eliot, 'The Mill on the Floss'

Undressing

Imagine a girl
shattered by a King's lust
heavier than an iron sky

imagine her
at the gates of an abbey

the cloth of surrender
ripped from the hollow of her throat.

Imagine how the Prioress
undresses this stranger
aroused by salt on pale skin

the way her young belly
must have spilt over him

her fragile body
slender legs, alabaster breasts.

A young lady's maid to Catherine of Aragon attracted the attention of Henry VIII. To evade his unwanted advances, she fled court to take sanctuary with Benedictine nuns near Reeth in Swaledale.

Waiting with Demeter for hand-over

I see Demeter first
in Tibshelf services
sipping tepid froth
marooned
by tables and travellers.
She meets
my half-smile.
Small talk
is an anchorless boat.

'Collecting my daughter'
'Halfway point'

Her eyes on the swell
of every question
sail to the sliding door
return, remote
as though rough seas
have blown her
onto fallow land
to mourn
temptation.

Growing pains

We lived
in white spaces
at the edge of print
wore our labels
on binary skirts
too short
too long
where mother police
divided us
into good girls
bad women
and defiant hearts
lost many battles
trying to write
our own names.

Inspired by the words of Margaret Atwood

Finding a voice

In the summer of 77, she was a flame
ignited with freedom, first time abroad
dropped into a family somewhere in August
with a girl not quite her age,
smoked her first cigarette, turned up the volume
on Presley and Bowie with those bolder boys,
burning ego in her yellow cheese-cloth shirt
fifteen with attitude, sweet enough to get by.
It was the Tuesday she fell in love
Il est mort, Elvis est mort
news blazed, breaking death with familiar songs
films dubbed falsetto, the discovery French Elvis
spoke in a way that could never be The King,
a lover's voice is a different country.

The girl we all wanted to be at school

She was a firefly
to our moths
Frida Kahlo's art
an internal rhyme
a haiku
kicking us out of her class.
After she left
I bought a maxi dress
wooden beads
strung silver on my thumbs
discovered
wearing yourself inside out
is much more than style.

Village school c1910

Rows of sorrow-grey
sepia scowls
assorted children
lined like sparrows
without a song
a cenotaph
scribed with faces
as if the teacher
has already taught them
the future will be counted
in who died
who survived.

Grandmother's war

After the war did you dig this soil
iron-rich with the blood of a brother, a lover

cut the earth sod by sod
turning clay pipes, buttons, a razor

the soles of dead men's shoes

stand in the trench of your potting shed
pruning, pricking out, wilting

fearing the nausea of spring-shoots
their trauma pushed towards light

releasing a shin bone, collar bone, thigh.

Monday 11th November 1918

Born from the same bones
I find you on Armistice Day

as the guns set down their agony of war
you surrender to Spanish flu.

In your sediments
I search for a novel.

The one about layers of lives
how history is never a fossil

how we use it to build
re-build stories
to become ourselves.

Still life

Grandmother's jug poured cream
in slow tears.
On most days the jug sat
locked in a mahogany case
behind glass we were not
allowed to touch.

Her glazed face
fragile bone
we never kissed
for fear of the hairline crack
and the weeping
that would pour from it.

Wife

For Annie, born 1929

Red was the colour of beginnings
the dress worn for their first dance
a song now filled with rain.
Watch how the sequins fall
from their jive, jitterbug, waltz.
She longs to take off her keen-worn hands
the loose gold circle that binds her to this farm
bury them at the back of the wardrobe
alongside his blue-songbook eyes.
Lost between the Astoria and lambing shed
she mourns the girl
washes ewes' blood from her overalls.

Fences

In your wood-pile of memory
you watch him collect old stakes
barbed wire, build a scaffold
on which to hang his blockade.
Claw hammer, six-inch nails
secure the smallest gap
the persistent tap tap
long after she has made her retreat.

You close the field gate, trap
the words that hurt.

Later, as the kitchen chokes in silence
rail-straight, she irons his faded workwear
her eyes the colour of condensation
running down the inside of the windows.
He watches her from his chair, half minded
to read the Farmer's Weekly
half-minded
to begin mending.

Mothering

The lame ewe that was left behind
has given birth to a son
in the shelter of limestone
tucked into soft rush and purple moor-grass.
We had begun to trust one another
as her swollen belly bubbled,
limped in and out of untroubled
April mornings. Under fleece skies
sat together with wheatear, lapwing
talked of butterbur, hazel catkins.

When her time came
there was no need for concern
his body, the colour of blackthorn blossom
tucked into her side, both greeting
the soft warming of the month's end.
I watched her from a distance
once more sewing her thread
into summer on these hills
both of us caught
like wool in hawthorn.

Flock

Bringing the sheep down from the moor
we run alongside the dogs
sisters on the move   bent into hail
on a day that wears grey
raddle-painted tuppings
colour coded backsides in the north-cut wind

we shelter into winter

wait for spring   for the days
when all we can talk about is birth
lambs on our tongues
gimmers   tups   slipping the wombs
new lives shadowing ours
born from this soil   breathing these fells

until   you tell him you are leaving

and all he can offer   is a crack of broken sun
slow skies closing over dry-stone walls
he says   we are all dreamers
even the ewes walk with the stars
watch the blood-moon rise
whilst their bellies fill with this path.

Day of awakening

Landrovers swagger into the stack yard
spilling shearers
tattooed with testosterone.

Fresh from school, skirts hitched
ties abandoned, the casual seduction
lingers over wool,

the ewe upturned
his clippers severing her.
Done. Fleece thrown into a corner.

Released
she runs to escape the persistent hum
of the blade on flesh.

Building resilience

I can never do cartwheels
the floor usurps
all these wayward limbs.
'You're not built for the gym'
father's voice bounces
off the walls
as I backflip from the beam
just to defy him.
Bowing to the crowds
the judges display a row
of perfect tens.
I keep this victory close
in case I need it another day.

Requiem for Gillian

His song snags your voice on the wires of a summer,
we lie on the lawn, soles kicking the sun to Roxy Music
dreaming up plans to kidnap Brian. I taste the cherry balm
that sweetens our lips, crushed by the brilliance of love.
We make a vow *Let's stick together*, whoever wins his heart.

And here you are today, stepping out through the radio
in white platform shoes, the red dress of a rock chick
and a figure I would have died for.

'Let's Stick Together', cover version of the 1962 original, released by Brian Ferry in 1976

Backpacking

The designer coat in the window
on Via Gesu
speaks perfect English
no translation needed.

We stroll into the Four Seasons
kick the kitten heels
of cash rich Signora into ugly verbs,
to covet, to envy.

Eat gelato al cioccolato
in the Galleria Vittorio Emanuele
re-apply lipstick in a boutique mirror
despite the assistant's bright red full stop.

Listen to poets in the Piazza del Duomo
on war, mutilation, racism, trafficking
gather their words together
to carry home in parentheses.

Breakfast in Brussels

We share the baker's table
a hum of warm bread
drifting across pine
two boats of coffee
strangers keeping silence
islands cut off by weather
when February breaches the door.
I notice you nod to customers,
greeting a girl
your smile speaks words
I would like to take home.
I glance over my glasses
count the croissants
the baton loaves
admire their neat rows
ask if you can pass the sugar
in my best French.
As you get up and leave, I wish
we had crossed the narrow sea
that divides us.

Lost

The brown leather glove
you drop
beside my blue door
does not speak of love
but keeps the shape of you close
so I can slip the yellow courage
of a hand inside
touch the red glow of my blush.

Proposal

When you leave, take me with you
I have been practising flight all summer
exercising my wings beside yours
storing up energy, scooping low over fields
learning to map-read, recognise clouds
stratus, cumulus, sleeping on southerlies.

Let's Christmas together
deep in South Africa
make it an adventure
teach me the language of air.

Joy

guilded Vienna
the afternoon
we shone
under the spell
of Beethoven
the shimmer
of immortality.

If only
we had known
we held an orchestra.

Truth or dare

Streetlamps cast across the ceiling
    play demons with our minds
first to bury their head under the sheets.
    This is our game.

Two boys at the Youth Hostel
    persuade us to join them in the bar
apple cider tastes of secrets
    the day you promise
never to tell me a lie.

I watch your backpack
    disappear onto the train
regret unravels
    postcards speak of places
we will never visit.
    I use your words to hide behind.

Adamas

Striding into the pub
his chariot
parked outside
carbon wheels
for this god of fire
cutting our light
into perfect love
a cubic frame
a jewel
on any girl's arm
but he chose mine.
Diamonds like him
are never forever
clarity and cut
lustre grey
boys and their baubles
the colour of bruises
yellow, black, blue
never transparent.

Rot in the Garden of Eden

The apple tree
we planted
is unpicking

as daylight
stitch by stitch
forsakes the flesh

apples hang
like hearts
without a body

pulped shapeless
the colour
of our canker

Green, how I wanted you

At first, I liked the sound
of you in my hair
words found on trees
before your colour rained
and the wall bruised my back.
Your eyes were friends
until every skin I wore
was not enough.
Your hand sown
into every day.
Even July was angry.

Title taken from the words of Federico Garcia Lorca, 'Romance Sonambulo'

Cuckoo

Listen.
My song echoes over April.

You know my tricks
to still your voice.

You retire to nest
weave shoots knuckle-tight

before my savage greed
expels you.

Remember other springs
when your sky cracked

broken by the distance
I would fly to steal you.

Listen.
You are my echo

with no song
of your own.

Silversmith

don't pretend
the silversmith
is not shaping you
into winter

he discards
your coat
rolls up his sleeves
hides from light

until all is sheet metal

the silversmith
snips hoary patterns
his fingers
filigree your bones

lingers in shadows
denies you gold

Cultivated

He gives you pearls
knotted on a string
you know they are alive
each night you listen to their sorrow
living in a box
at the bottom your dressing table drawer.
They weep for the salt of the sea
wrapped between dry tissue paper
you dream you set them free.
His necklace sleeps tight against your neck
breathing pearl breath
whilst you
lie trapped in starched sheets
dreaming of the sea.

Coercive

He buys me
an orange tree
because he can

picks a halo of sun
offers a topaz sea
all the sweetest flesh.

But his acid voice
assaults all choice

and behind the eyes
green round moons
of pith and rage

spit blameless words.
Oranges
are a vindictive fruit.

Violets

I have lived with you
just enough
to understand darkness.
We who are neither red nor blue
know the balance of each other
hold close to the ground
wear our hearts on the outside
both waiting
to see who will move first
release the toxic seeds
dark purple
destroy the other.

Letter home

I post in haste before ink dries.

<u>Underline</u>
bitter northerlies
argumentative springs
summers of accusations
autumns that aspire to more gold
than we can offer each other
winters that roll over into petulant days
listless when they fail to have their way.

We weather storms under this heavy slate
until there is no season I can write you into.

Wild swimming

In Budapest
she steamed my pores
scrubbed my skin

I was opaque
lost in incense
purged from the years I carried.

After the hammam
she left me with the river music
and I thought of the day

we climbed fells
stumbling upon the isolation
of a cool tarn.

How we plundered that pool
immersed our egos
scoured our hearts.

After
we lay side by side
listening to the other, drowning.

Black-dog day over Iona

West at Sliabh Meadhonach
an island forgets
it is an island
glens cling to their interiors
mountains take prisoners
every rock a cave.

You ask is there an English name
for this Great Loneliness
I call it a scorpion
in a desert of stones
a cell without a door
in a wall of days.

Release

Last night
we lay on the lawn
watched the flower moon
a Chinese whisper
blown into a stain of ink.

Tomorrow
I will untie all the words
we nearly shared
free them from their truth
their lie.

Therapy

I sit opposite her knees
avoid the eyes.
Her walls are sterile.

She speaks deliberately
as though she knows
I feel a fraud.

Sometimes I look up.
Behind her head his face
carved into the bark of a tree.

There's safety in the forest.
I have cultivated every sapling
between yesterday and tomorrow.

I would have climbed over her
to touch his mouth
but I no longer see the features.

Now all trees look the same.
Did he wait for autumn
bones of branches picked clean.

Every Tuesday I visit.
Her eyes are walls
and I am sterile.

Empress's new clothes

dark blue velvet
cut from 60s rock
Carnaby Street
embroidered into every seam
Quant Queen
of the vintage shop
high on borrowed Chanel No 5
a dress to hide inside
wear another woman's story

Banished

For the nuns who once lived on Iona

Robina is a summer garden now
a dandelion that seeks April
she drifts alongside haar
nests high with the rooks
rests in this granite shelter
beside St Ronan's Chapel
her worn tombstone
breaks a lawn of daisies

she watches over the Sound
towards the Isle of Women
sisters cast out across salt

Al Khor

In the spit of a city
my oil stained water
rises with the sun
over glass-lined skies
minarets and wind towers
washes the Gulf,
bears the weight
of slack-backed dhows
bellies full of black lemon
sana leaf, saffron
sailing the centuries
from sand into concrete
a snake shedding skin.

After dusk, I dream
with the Bedouin,
lap against the stars
named after their camels
flow alongside
the ebb and fall
follow myself back
to beginnings.

Al Khor, in Arabic, the creek

Alchemy

Instead of the Spice Bazaar
I want to show you
Aya Sofya, Blue Mosque,
the Basilica Cistern
but in a sudden turn
between two mosques
prayers snag the scents
of mulberry, mimosa,
rose irani, mango,
sumac, cardamom
crystals of eucalyptus
hand to mouth corners
aflame with paprika,
the pestle and mortar
of everyday lives
crushing up against us.

Guilt

I should never have read you the fable of *Icarus*
it was always the mother's fault, allowing her child to melt.

I touch your face in the sea, smell judgement on your breath
our eyes meet, offer no answer, I want to say, 'Can I hold you?'
give you my wings, explain flight is not always about leaving.

When I told you the story of a boy,
I whispered south winds, thermals, red skies
floated in the debris of my lie

betrayed you to the sun
watched as you faltered
until falling was the only word we shared.

Beachcombing

You trap
the butter shells
where your sister
holds secrets in sand.
Their rice light
is porcelain
each salty spit
a tiny womb
holds everyday words
born from the sea
in a tight fist of pain.

To a daughter on forgiveness

Every day I anchor you close
into the curves of weak flesh.
You, believing I dance purple
over the bones that break us.
My sins are an overcoat
woven into your skin.
I am chained to your path,
every minute, you, my air
every second, me, your breath.

Child of Montmartre

you wear this city on your tongue
its fabric wraps your body
stretches the eighteenth arrondissement
hip and blowsy
inhabits the wholesale shops
with buyers from ASOS
exiles at home

chic stranger
dusting French off your textiles
you flirt with the garçon
he lights your cigarette
heads almost touching
when did you start to smoke

under the shift of November
the Eiffel Tower speaks of secrets
a bar in Bastille hides early snowfall
we run through the slush
slip   on the eggshells of each other's shoes
find a backstreet cafe laced into a bodice of vines
sit   drink red wine

I know I must let you go

Butterfly

You time how long it takes
to fasten her into silk
fifty-five ivory buttons
before she slips between your fingers
slides away into this January morning.

She reminds you
of the time you caught a White Admiral
so fragile it hurt to still the wings
and somehow feeling
it needed the whole sky.

Light seeker

My evening walk
towards solstice
cuts through air
so thick I want to sleep
beyond these shortening days.
But, for now,
I wrap sparse daylight
into gifts
to place beside the fire
under pine trees and baubles,
talk to lamps
that steal the afternoon,
tell them somewhere
in this fist of winter
is a fight that breaks
the glass of days.

If nothing is left that life can touch

I will lead you
to the Piazzale Michelangelo
watch you fade into the bells below
nudge against terracotta roofs
stir pinks and creams and half-golds
fires that trace the folds of Firenze.
The red brick dome
a lotus flower
will burst you open.

Autobiography

Abandon the poetry
of metaphorical uplands
edit out red grouse
            limestone
            ling
embrace stanzas
                                    outside the margins
rock similes
break shores
justify those darker verbs
conceal
engulf
expel.

Listen to the pen
when it drifts towards spits, cliffs,
speaks of erosion, backwash, tides.

Walking backwards from birth

It is the beginning
I am child

so easy to be this small,
lungs ghost

echo on frost-air
haunt the first breath,

light pinks, lifts
the ridge above the river
water releases flight,

beech womb-buds
seeds slip their spirits.

In the year
before I am born

you plant a holly tree
for protection.

Eulogy for a stargazer

I imagine you
at the far side of the universe
interstellar
floating in a lagoon
of your iridescent laughter
welcoming the birth
of new stars.
Galaxies will huddle
around the dust
of your journey
flux-trailing the night
when all I want to see
is your face in Venus,
the Pole Star
the Plough,
sky-markers
you taught me
before I had to search
this other world
where death implodes
and somewhere out there
I know you ride
a supernova.

Final destination

Drive me across the A66
seek those gentler peaks

we are done
touching sunrise

from aircraft seats,
camping in deserts

crowding up creeks
into spice-soured souqs

the sun branding
henna on skin.

Let us untie and unwind
our concentric lives

free what is left
to Atlantic winds

the wilderness carvings
of distant millennia

inhabit the slate-slack air.

Return to Linthwaite

I wake at Linthwaite and through the reeds
catch no reflection in the tarn

I am tethered grasses
bracken spindles uncoiling with decay

sing no sorrow.

Don't look for my face on distant fells
or catch the scent of familiar paths

I am home
come visit sometime.

Coniston Old Man

A width of lake
cracks this living rock
mountain on the wing
of deep water
a room with a mirror
two halves of you
dividing the sky.

Here, the deceit
of sun on stone
can stitch a torn mind.

She who sings is not always happy

Marthe longs
for her own bathroom
tomb-like isolation
a simple tiled space.
His gaze collides
in a monologue of pure lilac
ochre, a pool of lagoon blue.
Her unspoken voice
spills wide across his canvas.

She resists his colour
allows her edges to fade
into a stone-womb of water
hides the limbs that make her whole
keeps close the sun on blush cheeks.

In response to The Bath, 1925, Pierre Bonnard.
The title of this poem, and the collection, is inspired by the words in 'Pierre Bonnard The Colour of Memory' The C C Land Exhibition, Tate Modern, London 23 January – 6th May 2019

"I'm not afraid of storms, for I'm learning to sail my ship."
Louisa May Alcott

Acknowledgements

The cover image is from a painting by Swaledale artist Jill Eagle, *Steps Wood*, 2018, www.jilleagle.co.uk and reproduced for this book with many thanks. Steps Wood lies between Marrick Priory, mentioned in the poem "Undressing", and Marrick village. The flagged stone path, or causey, that runs uphill through the wood is known locally as the 'Nuns' Steps'.

A huge thank you to Alison Lock for writing the foreword. I am a great admirer of her poetry, www.alisonlock.com.

Many thanks to Kerry Darbishire for her kind words and support: www.indigodreams.co.uk/kerrydarbishire and www.handstandpress.net.

The Louisa May Alcott quote on page 63 is taken from *Women, Inspiring Quotes & Artistic Responses, Volume 1*, Wild House Publishing, 2019.

Previous publications:

- "Green, how I wanted you" and "Time machine" were first published in *New Contexts: 1*, Coverstory books, 2021
- "Waiting with Demeter for hand-over" was long-listed in Paper Swans Press Single Poem Competition 2020, and first published in an e-book at paperswans.co.uk
- "Still life" will be published in 2021 in the *Write on the Farm Anthology, Volume 2, Such a Place Exists*, Stramongate Press, Kendal
- "Cultivated" was first published in *The Dawntreader 039*, Indigo Dreams Publishing, 2017
- "Al Khor" was first published in *Well Dam, Poems for Parched Humans*, Beautiful Dragons Press, 2019
- "Return to Linthwaite" was first published in *The Dawntreader 034*, Indigo Dreams Publishing, 2016

Other notes:

- "Black-dog day over Iona" and "Banished" were written during Roselle Angwin's Iona, Islands of the Heart residential course, April 2019, roselle-angwin.co.uk/fire in the head
- "Requiem for Gillian" was written in memory of my childhood friend Gillian Nixon, nee Telfer
- "Walking backwards from birth" prompted by the line "It is not easy to be this small" from *Negotiations with a Volcano*, Naomi Shihab-Nye

Thank you to Angela T Carr @adreaming skin, for her 'poem-a-day' month-long online courses that helped bridge a difficult year in 2020. Several poems in this collection grew out of her inspiring prompts.

A special thank you to Jane Merritt for her hospitality and all her time spent with me discussing both poetry and our shared farming heritage.

To Geraldine Green, and all the members of the Write on the Farm group in Cumbria, for your friendship, support, and cakes, over the last few years. I must also include an additional thank you to Geraldine, and all her co-tutors at Brantwood, Coniston, for the many inspirational residential courses I have attended. The seeds of some of the poems in this collection were sewn in both settings. www.indigodreams.co.uk/geraldinegreen

Thank you to North Yorkshire Stanza, Brian Clark, Ian Gouge, David Smith and all the members of the group for your valuable comments on many poems, including some in this book.

Finally, to Mo, for his love and encouragement in all things 'writing'.

www.ingramcontent.com/pod-product-compliance
Ingram Content Group UK Ltd.
Pitfield, Milton Keynes, MK11 3LW, UK
UKHW040021200726
13854UKWH00001B/291

9 781838 232139